Heaven's Intervention On Earth

I0151514

DR. JULIE HITCHENS

Heaven's Intervention On Earth

Publisher: Dr. Julie Hitchens

Copyright © 2016 Julie Hitchens Ministries

ISBN: 978-0615921600

Printed in the United States of America

Scripture quotations taken from the New King James & King James Version. Copyright © 1982 by Thomas Nelson, Inc. Used by permission. All rights reserved.

No part of this book may be reproduced or transmitted in any form, or by any means, electronic or mechanical, including photocopying, recording or by any information storage and retrieval system without permission in writing from the author/publisher.

Author Dr. Julie Hitchens
www.juliehitchensministries.com
Cover Design:
Dr. Julie Hitchens

DEDICATION

I dedicate this work to my Almighty God that He might be glorified through my recount of His undying love for me through divine intervention on earth where he uses angels

To my husband Joseph and children, I love you. I thank you for all your hard work and dedication to this work of the Kingdom. When I felt like giving up you kept up the fight to endure to the end.

CONTENTS

FORWARD

It is such an honor to write the foreword for Heaven's Intervention On Earth because Dr. Julie Hitchens and I have worked together in Ministry for twenty years in Houston, Texas. She is a woman of character, a woman of holiness, a woman of truth and a woman of much insight and wisdom. Dr. Julie is not only my Apostle but she is my beautiful wife.

As I sat talking to my wife on many wonderful evening we would always share our childhood story's then we would most time began talking about how GOD had intervene in our lives. Heaven's Intervention On Earth is just part of the miraculous ways that Christ Jesus has showed Himself strong in Dr. Julie's life. Her stories truly exemplifies the love of the Father and how He is so willing to embrace our needs if we would just allow Him (Our creator) to be Father in our lives. She tells of how the LORD filled her gas tank with gas in her time of need, to miraculous healing, Angelic visitations and her visitations to Heaven. She tells how the Father gave her a message to never let the body of Christ forget the purpose of Christ life and death. All is because the Father's unfailing love for us.

ACKNOWLEDGMENTS

Heavenly Father thank you for always being there for me
and for all the miracles and angels you sent to help. Some I
know and some I do not know. You are so awesome and
I love you too.   All Glory To You!!

Chapter 1

ANGELIC BEINGS

This book is not to encourage you to worship angels, gifts, or miracles but to glorify God our Creator. Thank God for all He has placed here on earth for His children. I can only hope this book gives you hope and encouragement. If you never see an angel know this whether visible or invisible according to the book of Colossians 1:16 and 2 Kings 6:17 they are here on earth to carry out God plans for our lives. They are messengers of God. I pray you have an intimate relationship with God and know He really loves us all. When angels appear they sometime appear as men. Genesis Chapter 18 says, Abraham welcomed three angelic beings who appeared to be nothing more than travelers. In Genesis 19:1 we read that Lot is visited by two of these three angels

.

The Word "Angel" comes from the Greek Word Aggelos, which means, "Messenger." Angels are Gods messengers. The Hebrew word mal'ak also means "Messenger." Angels praise, worship and serve God just like we do. We are not to worship the angels but God alone. Angels were created by God and were created for many different purposes; to deliver messages from God to us, to deliver messages to God from us, guide us, protect us, minister to us, strengthen us, encourage us, and to deliver us and so much more. There are armies of angels serving God and doing Gods will. Angels are ministering spirits as referenced in the books of Hebrew 1:14 and Luke 24:37-39.

<u>Angels Appearance</u>

Angels are ministering spirits of God. They may be visible or invisible. They may appear in a manner as shinning in glory, a dazzling light, but they often take on the appearance of men or women. Like us angel were all created to be holy. Some angels have "fallen" because they rebelled against God, under Satan's leadership (Revelation 12:9). A fallen angel is a wicked or rebellious angel that has been cast out of Heaven.

Scripture References of appearances of angelic beings found in the Bible:

Ordinary people who carry messages Job 1:14; Luke 7: 24; Luke 9:52
Prophets Isaiah 42: 19, Malachi 3: 1
Priest Malachi 2:7
Church leaders Rev 1:20
Pillar of Cloud Exodus 14:19
Pestilence or Plagues 2 Samuel 24:16-17

Chapter 2

HEAVENLY PLACES

I know a man in Christ who fourteen years ago was caught up to the third heaven. Whether it was in the body or out of the body I don't know, God knows.
2 Corinthians 12:3

I can't tell whether in the body are not in the body, I do not pretend to totally be able to explain it. I do not know how it occurred or in other words how it was brought about. Whether my spirit was separated from the body or whether the scene passed before my mind in a vision.

What I know to be evident is that God has the power if He chose to transport the body to heaven and power to separate the soul from the body. He also has the power to present to the mind so clearly the view of the heavenly.

The Bible Speaks of Three Heavens

1. The aerial, including the clouds and the atmosphere, the heaven above us, until we come to the stars.
2. The starry heavens the heaven in which the sun, moon, and stars.
3. The heaven beyond the stars. That heaven was supposed to be the residence of God, of angels and of the holy spirits. It was this upper heaven, the dwelling place of God, to which Paul was taken. The region where God dwelt, where Jesus Christ was seated at the right hand of the Father and where the spirit saints or justified ones are assembled. **2 Corinthians 12:2**

Angels Names in the Bible

Angels
Archangel
Michael
Gabriel
Abaddon
Apollyon
Destroyer
Satan
 Demon
"Living Creatures"
Cherub or Cherubim
Seraphim
 Sons of God
Book of Revelation

Chapter 3

ANGELIC VISITATIONS

Divine Protection

When I was around age twelve or thirteen I would be home alone babysitting my sibling. My mom and her male friend would go out clubbing on the weekends. I would be up late nights waiting up for them to come home. I would be afraid that someone would break into our home to harm us while they were away. I would be so tired of trying to wait up for my mom and watching out for intruders. When I was afraid I would pray Lord I am so afraid and tired. One night I prayed and there appeared before me two small angels with wings near the windows and hover in the air in the bedroom. There was a peace that came upon me when they appeared. I heard rest and I fell to sleep. I don't know how long they stayed there or when they left.

Divine Protection

One night my mom and her live in friend was getting ready to go clubbing, before they left, my mom's boyfriend said to me go and make sure all the windows were locked. He had never me to do this before. I thought nothing of it I did as he said. Then he asked me did you make sure the windows were locked and I answer yes. Then right before he and my mom walked out the door he said he needed to use the restroom before they leave. He went to the restroom. When I passed through the hall by the restroom to go to my bedroom, I saw him taking a hand full of pills which was strange. I had never seen him take pill before and he wasn't sick or anything. So I was curious why he was taking pills. They left and I locked the door behind them. It was late so I put my sibling to bed and turned

5

the restroom and hallway lights on and I sat in the living room as usual waiting up for my mom to come back home. I tried very hard to stay up so I could hear them knock to open the door. If I didn't hear them knock at the door she would become angry and verbal abusive. (In my next book There Was Purpose in My Pain I talk about my life) Being tired I fell to sleep on the sofa and I was a waken by an (angelic) voice saying softly, Julie wake up. Then the angel said don't move, then I heard the angel say look toward the hallway. Moving my eyes not my body. I could see the lights in the hallway and restroom were off. I remembered turning on the lights and my sibling were too short to reach the light plus they were still sleeping. I could see a shadow of a person in the hallway looking around the corner wall. The light was shining through the thin curtains on the window in the living room from the outside street light in the community. I was afraid all I could see was this figure of a man. The angel gave me step by step instruction. I did exactly as I was instructed by the angel. The angel said when I tell you to turn the light on I want you to move quickly and take three giant steps and say calmly where is my mama. Next I heard the angel say move now! I did as I was told by the angel and when I turn on the light switch in the living room where I was it was my mom live in male friend, looking around the corner wall. My heart was racing fast but I stay calm and I ask him where is mama? He said at her friend house then he said lay back down baby and go back to sleep. I ask what friend? "He said down the street. So I open the front door and walked down the street to my mama friend's house and knocked on the door but nobody answered it was 3am. So I went back home but when I return home my mom male friend was gone. I wondered how did he get in because nobody let him in. When I turn on the lights switch in the hallway and restroom it didn't come on. My mom male friend had unscrewed the light bulbs from the socket in the hallway and restroom. He couldn't have gotten in from the front door because all locks were locked. That was the reason I slept on the sofa to unlock the door when they got home. I realized that when he said he was going to use the restroom he unlocked the restroom window with the intent to come back to do me harm of some sort. But God! The angel of the Lord protected me. God is good, thank you Jesus. I am grateful to the lord for all the times he helped me.

Emergency Protection

When I was 19 years old coming from work
I was driving 65 miles an hour home on the freeway. When my steel belt front tire blew out on my car. The car went out of control and did an unstoppable donut on the freeway. While spiraling out of control I saw my whole life flash before me in seconds like photos or a video. When I came out of the car spin I was going head on to traffic. I tried to hit my brakes and turn my steering wheel but it was locked. I began to pray Lord help me. Then all of a sudden the steering wheel unlock and the car straighten out but it was heading across the middle divider into the traffic on the other side of the freeway. No matter how I hit the brakes as I was going across the grass the car would not stop. Than all a sudden I hit the brakes the tires and rim dug in the ground just right before entering into coming traffic on the other side of the freeway. Two men driving an 18 wheeler truck stopped to help me. I stepped out of the car shaken but unharmed. My high heel sunk into the ground my heart racing with fear. My bible was in the back window of the car and one of the guys saw my bible and said you should have had your bible in the front window he smiled. Then he said because it's a miracle you are alive. I said thank you Jesus. Truly it was a miracle because it was nothing I could do to stop the car from spinning or going into the into coming traffic. The way my car stopped in the grass and dug in to the dirt it had to be God's super natural help!!

Miracles and Guided Footsteps

My first pregnancy my husband was not ready to have a child at the particular time. He told me we were too young for a child. We had not plan to conceive at that time. My husband had just gotten out of the military when we got married. His family members try to persuade me to have an abortion. I did not agree with that morally. I would hear them all out. After hearing them I would explained I was not going to abort the baby and why. I told them that I was scared of having a baby and didn't know what I was going to do but did know it was not going to be an abortion. Abortion was not an option for me. I don't know where I got such conviction but I stood firm despite all the pressure to have an abortion. I had many fears and mix feelings concerning the baby. I felt so alone during that time. I kept all of my doctor's appointments. I had Edema meaning swelling of the feet while I was pregnant and I had to walk long ways to catch a bus. My husband made it perfectly clear that if I had the baby I was on my own and that he absolutely was not going to help me take care of the baby.

Miracle

I carried the baby to term. My husband dropped me off at the hospital at night. I don't know how long he stayed or when he left. He never said bye. I didn't see him for another five days. After I gave birth perhaps he thought not to come back. I experienced complication use I would not dilate the centimeter needed. My labor was long it had been 24 hours. The baby was in distress. I walked and they use electron shock equipment and monitor the level of stress on the baby during the procedure. I still was not able to dilate the centimeters required to deliver the baby. This procedure did not help. Due to the urgency to save my baby the doctor decided to do a C-section. They roll me to surgery room I was afraid. The nurses begin prepping me for surgery and I prayed Lord you promised you would be with me. I don't want to have surgery please help me. The doctor began sterilizing my abdomen and I yelled the baby is coming!! The doctor said no he's not and I yelled yes he is!! The doctor looked and said oh, oh yes he is! His head is coming and they delivered the baby. God was on time it looked like He was not coming. He was on time!

Miracle After Birth

After I gave birth I got a very high fever and the doctor kept me in the hospital to watch me to make sure that I didn't get an infection. I got very depress because no one came to visit me. No one in my family not even my husband nor his family nor did any one call me. No one checked on me for five days. After the fever drop the hospital called my husband at home and at work but he was nowhere to be found. I went through a depression and fear.

What was I going to do with a baby? During my depression in the hospital I didn't go to see my baby. I was scared. On the third day a nurse came into my room and said we noticed you haven't gone to see your baby. Afterward on the fourth day I got the courage to go see him. I got more depressed because he was so tiny and I knew I now had someone who was depending on me for survival. But I had no job and no support. My husband made it clear that he was not going to help me. As I looked at my baby laying there in the nursey so cute and small. The nurse asked me if I like to have him brought to my room I told her yes. I was told I had a healthy baby boy. The moment I held my baby and I realize how much I loved him and I said I finally got somebody that will love me.

Joy After Birth

I held my baby and my sadness began to leave me. Although I didn't know what I was going to do I had a peace that God was going to work it out for me and my baby. After days they finally got in touch with my husband day five. When he came to pick me up I asked him where he had been and he said he was with his girlfriend. After we made it home he did nothing for me or the baby. I tell you this because the Lord came through for me again and again. After about three weeks, one night while I was asleep my husband packed his clothes and left me and my baby.

After Birth Provision

There was no money left for food, milk, pamper or to pay rent. I had no food in the house and just a few cans of formula and pampers. I sat on the sofa and cried and I prayed Lord I don't know what to do, I don't have a job, I don't have any money, I don't have no food, the baby barely had milk and pampers. I can't go home to my mom. I prayed as tears was rolling down my face I felt a sudden unction get the phone book and start calling the local churches to ask for help. None of it made sense at the time but I kept calling until the second or third church answer and I told them I need help. I explained to the person on the phone that I just had a baby and my husband left me. I told them my situation and a gentleman said someone will come to your home tomorrow and talk with you. An elderly white couple came over the next day and talked with me. I told them my situation and they told me they would be back in a little while. When they return it was only a few hours. This couple filled my pantry with food. They filled my refrigerator until there was no room in it. My baby had pampers and milk piled up in the closet. While writing this book I could barely hold back the tears. God has been good to me. Glory to the Lord he came through for me again. He used a little couple who had the heart of God. They were angels. I am Grateful for what they did for me a stranger. There's more they didn't stop there, they paid my rent up for three **months**. After several weeks I got my six-weeks checkup and I got a clean bill of health.

Favor

I kept praying lord I realize I have a little time to get a job before the rent will be due again. I didn't know where I would find a job or a babysitter. I had no income and no transportation. I start thinking about what I was going to do next.

I prayed to God and I said Lord I need a job but I don't know where to go plus I don't have no one to keep my baby.

While praying a thought came to my mind about the daycare in the apartment community. The daycare was privately owned. I walk over spoked with the director of the daycare. I told her my situation and that I needed help with my baby so I could find a job. The lady was old enough to be my mom. She asked me how long will you need me to keep him and I said just a couple of hours so I could fill out some applications. She said ok. I told her I would pay her a soon as I found a job and receive a pay check.

I didn't even have money to ride the bus I walk 3 miles looking for work in the business area of town. I kept walking until I got to a corner that had a Jack-In-Box Restaurant. I went in and asked the manager if they were hiring and he said yes we are and he hired me on the spot. I was so happy I walked back to the apartment and it seen like it only took ten minutes. When I made it back to the daycare I told the daycare director I found a job and she rejoiced with me. Her name was Mrs. Gaston the owner and Mrs. McGowan the director. I found favor with the owner and again God came through. Ms. Gaston eventually became like a mom to me and a grandma to my son.

Mrs. Gaston would keep my son for me after the daycare was closed so I could work over time. We work out a deal on my day off from my job. I would help her at the daycare. Ms. Gaston children were older but my son really enjoy them. I move away for the city but I just want to say Mrs. Gaston thank you so very much. God is good He surround me with people who care about me. I found favor at my new job at Jack in the Box. It wasn't long before I was promoted into management and was making a lot of overtime. This was only possible because of Ms. Gaston. I will share more in my book title (There Was Purpose in My Pain)

The Miracle that Kept Me Alive in The Darkest Hour.

I was so depressed about my life that I decided to take some pain pills and end it. I wrote a note, put my baby to sleep. After taking the pain pills I was sitting on the sofa waiting for the pills to take effect. I had a lot of emotional hurt and thoughts going on in my head. No one to talk to or advise me in marriage or as a mother. I felt so a shame for how I was treated. Suddenly I heard a voice say to me if you die who's going to take care of your baby?

The pain was deep I thought at the time my baby was better off without me. After hearing the audible voice ask me the questions. I thought to myself my son will not have any one to care of him just like me. My mom was abusive until I basically moved out and I never felt loved. Then I thought about my husband he didn't want no baby or nothing to do with the baby. After thinking things through my baby had no one. My next thought there is no telling when my husband would come home or if he would come at all. I got up and grab a phone and called the ambulance service. I spoke to a paramedic and told them what I did. The dispatcher said will you be able to open the door and let us in because if you can't we will have to call the police. I told him yes I would be able to open the door. When paramedic came and asked me what did I take I showed him the prescription. The paramedic explained to me that the pills I took would have killed me if I had fallen asleep. You see if it was not for the Lord using this audible voice to ask me those questions. I would have fallen to sleep. I fought to stay awake all night.

The Paramedic also explained that if they had taken me to the hospital the state would have filed charges against me and possibly taken my baby. But God step in again and show me mercy. The paramedic asked me if I had someone who could come and stay with me for the night to keep me awake. He also explained that I needed to walk around during the night to stay awoke and drink plenty of water. My husband older sister lived near me. I called her and she came right away. The paramedic talked with her and she took me and my son to her home. I was 19 years old. The next day I finally fell to sleep and slept for three days straight without waking up. God is good He saved my life and gave me another chance at life!

<u>Helping and Guiding Angels</u>

One night while I was sleeping, in a dream the angel of the Lord came to me and said for me to move to a city. Then I was shown the name of the street in the dream that I was to move to. He showed me the main road that I was to travel onto to get to the street but I didn't want to move away from my relative. So I contacted a realtor to show me some houses in the city I live in. I was resisting the move. Every house that was shown me the agent would say they have just leased it or a person would be leaving out of the house with the keys in their hands. I did not realize God was not giving me a choice. Everywhere I went the agent was told it just leased or no longer available. I thought I will take an apartment and started looking for an apartment. Not even apartment, None I could afford was available. After weeks and days of looking I went home and sat down and said ok Lord I don't know anything about the city or area where I'm going. I won't have a job when I go so what am I to do? This is why none of it made sense. I got tired of the doors closing in my face and said Lord you won. Okay how am I to do it and when am I to go. I drove to the city that was showed me in the dream and found the house with ease. It was a big beautiful bricked home with large bed rooms and a beautifully landscaped yard. I talked to the owner and she didn't even ask me if I had job that was a miracle. I didn't need a realtor, didn't have to fill out no forms or application. The owner took the rent and worked with me for the deposit and gave me the keys to the house that very same day. We move in that week. I started a registered home daycare. I baby sat and picked up children after school that was my job. With God's help I never miss a rent payment and I was only about an hour from my family. My children were happy. The Lord is amazing. Thank you Jesus!

Visitation in Heaven

In 2004 I was in prayer and I was caught up to heaven. As I walked into the throne room of God. I paid very close attention to details. Such as how I entered the room I walked in like a soldier. When I came before the Throne where Jesus was I got down on my hands and knees and bowed down before Him in Honor. When I rose up to my feet I said mission completed. When I looked at the jewel in my hand there were people from all nation inside of it. I looked at Jesus sitting on the throne and He had a crown on but no jewels in it. Then I heard the Father say the Son is worthy of the souls He was slain for. {Revelation 5:12} Then I went and put the jewel in Jesus crown. Then I heard the Father say the only thing you could ever give the Son is the souls He died for. The Heavenly Father said to me never let the people forget the only thing they can give Jesus is souls.

Messaging Angels
"Uncle"

Late one Saturday night a minister angel woke me up to pray for my uncle. I begin to intercede on the behalf of my uncle until I felt a relief. Later on that Sunday morning I spoke with a family member and was told my uncle whom I was praying for had been out drinking. While driving his motorcycle home he had a bad wreak. He was scratched up very badly and had road burns on his body but he survived the accident. Praise the Lord!

Messaging Angels
" Brother "

One Friday night around one o'clock in the morning I was awakened by an angel of the Lord to pray for my brother. I heard he is in danger I jump out of bed and got down on my knees and cried out for my brother. I prayed until I got a relief that he was ok. When morning came I called my mom to find out where my brother new address so I could visit him. He had move to a new apartment and nobody knew his new address they only knew the area of town he lived in. So I went looking for him in the area I was told.

I drove around the area and then the Lord instructed me drive to the back of the apartments and it was there that I saw my brother coming out of his back door. I yelled his name to get his attention and he asked me how I knew where he lived. I told him God show me. I explained to him that I was awaken in the nigh to pray for Him. This is why I came looking for him. He started crying saying I went looking for a guy last night to kill him because he had been lying on me. My brother took his gun and rode the bus to find a guy but he couldn't find him. I told him the Lord showed me that if he had found the man it was going to be him that was going to be killed. Thanks to God He turned it and my brother didn't harm anyone or lose his life that night. Hallelujah!!!

One Friday night around one o'clock in the morning I was awakened by an angel of the Lord to pray for my brother. I heard he is in danger I jump out of bed and got down on my knees and cried out for my brother. I prayed until I got a relief that he was ok. When morning came I called my mom to find out where my brother new address so I could visit him. He had move to a new apartment and nobody knew his new address they only knew the area of town he lived in. So I went looking for him in the area I was told. I drove around the area and then the Lord instructed me drive to the back of the apartments and it was there that I saw my brother coming out of his back door. I yelled his name to get his attention and he asked me how I knew where he lived. I told him God show me. I explained to him that I was awaken in the nigh to pray for Him. This is why I came looking for him. He started crying saying I went looking for a guy last night to kill him because he had been lying on me. My brother took his gun and rode the bus to find a guy but he couldn't find him. I told him the Lord showed me that if he had found the man it was going to be him that was going to be killed. Thanks to God He turned it and my brother didn't harm anyone or lose his life that night. Hallelujah!!! Prayer!!!!

Urgent Pray for My Husband"

One Sunday I was in church praying at the altar then I heard this urgent request pray for my husband, he is in danger. I prayed until I got a release in my spirit. Shortly after I made it home from church my husband came home. He had been working a side job cutting trees and he got in an argument with the guy who was hauling the branches to the dump yard. He told me that the guy demand more money. My husband said as he walked away the man pull out a gun to shoot him in the back but a couple of workers that were with them grab the guy with the gun. They stop the man from shooting him in the back. He said he looked back and the other workers were wrestling with the guy over the gun and he got in his truck and drove off. God save his life that day.

Pray! Pray! Pray!

Angelic Defense

In my earlier days when I open the doors to a new church for the first time. I had an evangelist speak for three nights that I had met at a store. He brought with him his wife and a friend. When he entered the church he had a different presence about him than when I spoke with him before the engagement. It really made me uncomfortable. I had not notice earlier that he had a spirit of control. I sat quietly while the Evangelist preached and I observe. I prayed the whole time and I heard the Spirit of the Lord say be not afraid you are not alone. I looked around the church and there were tall angels standing side by side as a hedge around the church. They step out and a glow of light was around them and then they faded away. The evangelist preached his message and told the people how the prophets were not important in the church. Afterward he called the people up for healing I remember this one young man was there that I saw a dream. In the dream an angel ministered to me about him and told me he needed healing.

When the evangelist called forth those who need healing I notice this young man did not stand up to get in line for healing. I asked the Lord why didn't he get up if he's sick and needs healing. The Spirit of the Lord said I told you to pray for him. God assigned certain people to help others. I waited until the guest speaker was finish and I told the young man what God had revealed to me in the dream about him needing healing in his blood. His older brother jumped up out of his seat and starting shouting and crying he said I know the Lord reveal this to you. He stated we did not share this report from the doctor with anyone not even our parents. Their parents were Pastors. I prayed for the young man and God healed him just like he said he would. The young man has his own family now and is living for the Lord. I then told the congregation you see the prophets are needed in the church just as Ephesians 4:11 says. If the Lord had not reveal this young man situation to me he would have never been healed that night. After that the guest speaker bowed his head down and his shoulder dropped. All the pride went right out of him. God did a miracle for that young man. Glory to the God!

<u>Angel Deliverance & Spiritual Warfare</u>

I experience spiritual warfare at a degree that I did not understand and the attacks were coming from areas that seemed like everywhere. I felt bound and oppressed. I cried out to the Lord for help day in and day out. Then one afternoon I saw a vision of a huge Angel and I heard. Praise the Lord, move your feet and hands. Resist the devil don't let him bound you, fight back. I started to move my feet, I began to jump around, I started running in place and I lifting my hands. The Angel I saw said walk where I walk and I will lead you out. In the vision it was like a forest or a jungle with so many trees, thickets and tall grass. As I looked down at the feet of the angel in the vision there were huge foot prints left behind him. I understood the Lord was leading me out of that place. It was about 30 days and I started a tent ministry winning souls for Jesus Christ. The battle came to stop the work of the lord. God delivered me.
Hallelujah!!

Angelic Protection

Years ago there were witches and warlocks that came to attack me in the church. I didn't know that my life was in danger because the Lord had not reveal it to me. While I was in the pulpit preaching I heard the Spirit of the Lord say to me look up and I did. There appeared a huge angel in the ceiling stretch over the pulpit area. I was instructed to stand under the angel and not to move from that place. After I preached I had everyone to come to me if they desire to be prayed for. I obeyed and stay there and pray for those who came up for healing and deliverance. While I was praying for other this one lady that was sitting in a chair in the middle isle fell out of her chair in to the middle isle. When I saw her she had mucus coming out of her mouth and was beginning to turn gray. I knew she was dead. There was no life. I prayed Lord please don't let her die. After I prayed for her the woman took in a deep breath and begin to move. After service I went to her and talk to her, she confessed to me that she was a witch. She said how could she not do witchcraft when she had been taught all her life. I learned that day how important it is to obey God's instructions through the Holy Spirit. Glory to God for all the His protection!!

Angelic Assistance

My family and I went to Columbus, Ohio to take an offering in person and to visit my pastor. We travel 1100 miles. We made it there fine but on the way back we had trouble with the alternator but we did not know it at the time. The lights in the dash was very dim and next no lights at all. We were between Missouri going toward Arkansas. I told my husband look down there is no light in the dash. We were talking and did not realize the engine was not running. I look out the window and there were angels on the back of the van on both side flying pushing us from the back top of the van. I told my family to praise God for what He was doing. The speed never changed on the freeway and we did not know there was no engine running. We all praised. The angels must have pushed us for about five miles before we were given instruction in what to do. I heard the spirit of the lord say to tell my husband to go to the nearest Wal-Mart to get a new battery so I told him.

This is where we brought the battery from. It was early morning hours as we travel. We made it to the Wal-Mart about 3am no one was in the automotive department so my husband asked for a manager who help him. They gave us a new battery and we drove to the next city on the freeway and the van lights started flicking while on the freeway the dash went dark gain but the van never lost speed of 65mph. I praise and prayed than I heard the spirit of the Lord said to tell my husband to turn off the freeway right here. I told my husband what I heard in the spirit and he follow the instruction. We did not know where we were but, when he steered off the freeway it took us to a little country road. It was dark and once we made there the van shut off. We sit there until the break of day then we could see a little store up the road.
Our van stop again we prayed then we remember we had a can of emergency battery charge booster that if we put it in the cigarette lighter and connect to batter it would charge the battery. The car started up again. My husband went in and ask the store clerk where was the nearest automotive store, they told him so we head back on the freeway. We drove just a few minutes before we had to pull over on the shoulder of the freeway again.

Little did we know it was just where we need to be for helped. My husband walked down the side of the shoulder of the freeway to get off the freeway on to the feeder road. Once he made it down to the feeder there was a store and little community there. He went in the store and a few minute me and the girls decide to get out and do the same. We got out of the van and went to the neighborhood store while walking there a lady in the community shout out to us do you need help. I yelled yes we need a taxi cab. The lady called a taxi cab while we wait at the store. This was in a little country town in Arkansas. The cab driver was very nice. He took us back to the van and waited on my husband to take the alternator off the van. He then took us all to the automotive store and back to the van no extra charge. My husband fixed the alternator and we made it home safely. God is so awesome and we prayed that this young man whoever he was if ever he needed anything that God would do it for him. Thank you lord!!

Angels do Warfare

Our ministry went through some spiritual warfare against witches and warlocks coming against the ministry. I still remember the exact day because the lights flicker off and on and the whole congregation stood up at the same time looking toward the entry door of the church as it opened by itself. The angels were warring when it was over the whole church sat back down at the same time. It was synchronized how we all stood and all set back down no one told anyone to stand or sit before or afterward. We continue with service as usually. God will protect His people from unseen dangers.
He is a good Father. Glory!!!!

Angels are with us on Earth

When I was given away at five years old to my great aunt I experienced angelic visitation. The day my great aunt came to select who she was taking to live with her. I didn't know her. My mother and dad had separated after the death of my sister. My mother did not tell us she was giving one of us away to my great aunt. She explained we would be spending the night. My mother lined us all up in a line from youngest to the oldest. I was standing at the end of the line and I heard a voice say she is taking you with her, my heart was racing with fear. I turned and look down with sadness and said inwardly I don't want to go with her because I don't know her. As I turned and was looking down I could see an angel standing at my right side. My aunt came to the end of the line after looking at my other siblings and said this is the one and I almost pass out. My heart raced within me. My mother then came over to me and said you will only spend a night. She will buy you some clothing tomorrow and bring you back. It was not the truth. The next day my great aunt told me my mother had given me to her. My heart was broken and my world spiral before me which left me with no peace about the way it was done. I would cry every day and night in private. I would lay awake praying. I look beside my bed and there was an angel sitting in a chair beside my bed every night for about a year. It took me that long to accept I was not going home. After I came to peace with the changes I no longer saw the angel at my bed. Grateful for all the Lord has done to comfort me.

<u>Angel Protect and Saved My Life</u>

I remember it was in the summer time and my parents were trying to reconcile their marriage and one day my sister Diane and I went to the store for my mother. I don't remember what it was for. I was seven and my oldest sister was eight. We were on our way back from the store getting ready to cross the highway when my sister step onto the highway then back to the side walk. Then she decided to go again and this is when she ran across the highway but I was still standing there not sure if I should go or not. We would always go across together but because of the way she did it I hesitated. She was standing on the other side of the highway waiting for me. I then looked up toward the balcony and I could see my parents gesturing with their hands and yelling something I got nervous. I thought I was in trouble because I didn't cross the road with my sister. I couldn't hear them and I didn't see the eighteen wheeler truck because I was trying to figure out what my parents were saying. Out of fear I didn't look for traffic I just starting running toward my sister. After I got in the middle of the road I looked to my right and there I saw an eighteen wheeler coming down the highway traveling fast.

I realized I couldn't get to the other side of the road in time nor could I go back to the other side where I ran from. So I just stood there frozen with fear in the road. Right when the eighteen wheeler was about to hit me an angel appeared and picked me up and tossed me on the side of the road. I landed on top of a street drain. The truck driver slammed on his breaks, jumped out of his truck crying and people were jumping out of their cars running to me. I was getting up off the ground dusting off my legs when the man was saying I'm so sorry for hitting you. I tried to stop with tears running down his face. I said you didn't hit me. He said yes I did, I said no you didn't. Then my parents came running over to me. The ambulance was called and they rush me to the hospital. No one listened to me I kept telling them the man didn't hit me. At seven I didn't know how to explain that an angel had picked me up tossed me to the side of the road and that what the truck driver hit was the angel instead of me. While at the hospital the truck driver came walking down the hall with a baby doll in his hand. He kept telling me how sorry he was and he told my parents how sorry he was for hitting me. I told him you didn't hit me but no one listened to me. I was release from the hospital that day to go home with no injuries. God spare my life and I am grateful!

<u>Angels Protection and Instruction</u>

There was a man that lived across the street from my dad who came and knocked on the door. I saw him talk to my dad outside a few times. I was twelve years old during this time. I answer the door and said who it is. He said his name and that he was from across the street. I yell to him and said my dad's not home. He said open the door. I repeated my dad is not home. Then he came to the side of the house to the window near the carport where the kitchen was and said open the window. I said no my dad is not home. Then he punched out the window pane and was trying to get his arm and hand in to open the window latch. My sister was one year younger than me and brother two years young than me. They both ran and got under the dinner table. Then I heard a voice say to me if he gets in you can't stop him from over powering you. Then I looked around and over in the corner was a wooden table leg which had not been there before. I ran and grabbed it and begin hitting his hand but he kept trying to reach the latch. There was blood all over the window and floor where he cut himself. He had gotten his arm in all the way to his elbow. I just kept hitting him until he finally pulled his arm back and left. The lord was with us!

Ministering Angels

Many years ago I was being ordained and license as an evangelist at my home church. There was about 500 people at the church at time, I was nervous. I heard the spirit of the Lord speak and say stay in the spirit or I will leave you ashamed. I didn't understand totally what He was saying but when I would focus on the people I would lose thought of what I was saying for a moment but when I stayed in the spirit I did not see their faces clearly and I would only repeat what I heard the spirit say. Lives were changed that night. Many gave their lives to Christ. I notice an angel with white wings standing by me in the service. There was one particular a man who had a dream that he did not understand and in my message a word was spoken that gave him clarity. He joined the church that night. When I would come out of the spirit I would hear get back in the spirit. All fear was lifted. To God be the glory!

Hospital Angelic Presence

My mother went in the hospital form complication of dialysis. The Doctor kept her in the hospital. I went to see her and there was an angel across the room near a chair in her room. I felt a sense of peace while in the room. I comb my mother's hair at her request. My husband and I had to leave shortly after. When we got down the hall a few steps I heard a voice say I would not see my mother this way again. I stop and thought about what I heard. I did not want to go but my husband had to work the next morning and we only had one vehicle working at the time.

When I got home I call the hospital to let my mother know that I had made it home and I ask how she was doing. She said ok and explained she was waiting on my brother who was coming to see her after he got off work. She also told me that she was going to call her sister. We said goodnight and I told her I would see her tomorrow. After getting off the phone with her I heard go to bed tonight for tomorrow your mother will need you. So I laid down and went to sleep. The next morning my husband was leaving for work he asked me, do you want to take me to work and keep the van? I told him no and that I will wait for him to get off and then go back out to the hospital. My husband was leaving for work and I heard go with him and keep the vehicle for your mother is going to need you. So I yelled to my husband wait! I need to go with you and keep the van, he said ok get dress. When we got to his job he got out the van I crossed over to drive off and I heard before driving of the parking lot call the hospital and I call my mother "she said hurry Julie it does not look good". My heart was racing. I called my brother who was close to the hospital, I ask him could he get there since he was closer and I explained to him I was on my way and that there was construction on the freeway in my area. While still sitting in the parking lot at my husband's job I called him and told him that my mom told me to hurry it was not looking good. My husband took off work and drove me to the hospital. When I got there my mother was sitting on the bed and my brother was there with her. She looked at me as to say is its time. I heard in the spirit to keep calm don't cause her to fear. So I smiled and ask if she was in pain. She told me yes and she asked me to be sure they did not put a catheter in her neck because my sister died after an intern at the hospital put a catheter in her neck and punched her lung.

I understood her fear of having one put in her neck. and I told her I would make sure it was not done. Time went on and things turned for the worst. My mother understood it was her time to go. A peace came on her as she told me it was over. But I call the family together and prayed for her healing. God did not answer our prayer the way I hope. I didn't want my mom to see me cry so I went into the bathroom in waiting area and prayed, Lord I am not ready for her to go. I heard the spirit of the Lord say pull yourself together for death to you is not as it is to the world. I dried the tears from my eyes got myself together and went back into the waiting room. They were telling me it was no use. All that day and into the night things got worst. My mother's pastor came to the hospital to be with the family about 7pm. My siblings and I took turns sitting with my mother. Early the next morning my mother's heart stopped and they resuscitated her. Finally the doctor came into the waiting area and said he needed to talk with the family on what we want them to do if her heart stops again. He explained sometime today she would pass. I call all my siblings, nephews and nieces together and explain to them that we had to make a decision on what to do. None of them were ready to release her but I remembered my mother telling me one day when I was younger sitting on her steps at her home that if she ever got to a place that the doctors couldn't help her, she would prefer to go on and not be a problem to anyone. I step in the hall to prayed again what was best for my mother and shortly afterward one of my sister came running down the hall and through the double doors shouting let her go, just let her go. So I told my siblings we were holding my mother here and that she would not go until she knew we were okay. After we agreed to let her go and my nephew and I signed the papers. Before the doctor stepped out of the waiting room over the hospital intercom we heard code blue and they called the doctors name. He came back a very short time later and said she had expired. While standing in the hospital hall waiting on the funeral home to come get my mother's body my mother's pastors and my husband were talking. I stood there but off to myself. One of the Pastor turned to me and said don't worry she was saved. My mother pastors said she gave her life to God months ago and was filled with the Holy Spirit. Boy what a peace came over me. The pastors were telling me how after one Sunday service she told them she wanted to be filled with the Holy Spirit and was not going to leave until she got filled. The greatest miracle was that my mother had accepted Jesus Christ as her savior. They told me the story how she was filled with Holy Spirit and afterwards told all our family that was there at church with her that whatever they do they need to get what she just got and how she felt. While they were still speaking, I heard my name being called, I turned to my right and an angel and my mother stood beside me. I could see them in the realm of the spirit and heard my mother voice say to me get the car keys from one of my sister and give the car to my baby brother. My baby brother was not present when she passed away. It was beautiful what I had seen next I saw the angel and my mother walk down the hall and then disappear. Shortly afterward I told my sister what I was told and she asked me how I knew she had the keys and the car. I explained to her what I was told and I told her how I was told.

Favor to Bury My Mother

We were preparing my mother's funeral and had very little money. On the insurance my mother had only $2,500. I didn't have the money to bury my mother so I prayed, Lord help me to give her a proper burial. I went to the funeral home and spoke with the owner and the Lord touch this man's heart and showed me favor. He was the Funeral Home owner he told me whatever I needed he would do. He said I could have any casket for her that he had and the price was not a problem. I pick the casket that I wanted with a price of $12,000,00. He paid for the police escort and limousine for the family, dinner at the wake. We held the wake in the city at the funeral home and the funeral in her home town. The burial ground was given to us by my mother's sister who had an extra family plot. I did not have enough money for the lining for the grave so I called a meeting with the sibling and we came up with the extra $700.00 needed. A bakery donated bread and cakes, people brought food for afterwards. The lord heard my prayers and answered. Hallelujah!!

There was an angel that stayed with me until everything was finished. I got everything I needed with what little I had. God answered my every prayer. My mother had a little restaurant she had rent for her business after being sick. She didn't make much there but manage to keep it open and stay busy. So we were having the after funeral dinner there, we went there before the funeral to clean it up and prepare the steam table for food as well as receive items that were being drop off by family and friends. While cleaning, all of a sudden the music in juke box started playing and no one put money into the machine. The volume got louder and louder. We all looked at each other. Then I looked at the clock which was above the junk box and I realized it was time to get to the church. Mind you the service was not schedule to start until 11am but one of my family members decide to start earlier without telling me. If the juke box had not played the music we would have missed the funeral. When we got there, there was no more seats. My mother was well known in the city. People were saved and healed that day. Just the way I believe my mother would have wanted it.

Chapter 4
MIRACLES

When I was a young girl my baby brother at the time was about three or four years old and he couldn't walk but he was able to crawl. I heard my great aunt and another lady talking about him not being able to walk. They said if his mother would bath his legs in dish water after washing dishes he would be strengthen in his legs and begin to walk. After moving back in with my mom I remembered what she said so one morning after washing dishes I picked my brother up and sat him on the edge of the sink and put his legs in the sink after washing dishes using the water to bath his legs. I prayed a prayer than I said to him you are going to walk. I did this twice and each time I prayed to God and said to my brother you're going to walk. In about two weeks he was pulling up on the sofa and coffee table and began standing then taking steps. I kept working with him for several days and he got up and was walking all over the house. I do not believe the dish water had anything to do with his walking. I truly believe it was my faith that God used, the dish water was a contact of my faith to strengthen and heal his legs. I know God heard my prayer as a child and gave my brother a miracle in Jesus name.

Miracle Intervention

I was told I could not have no more children after my 1st because my tubes were block. Test was being run when I conceive my 2nd Child. I didn't have insurance to go to a hospital even though I went to a doctor until it was time to have the baby. I kept all my checkups. I had to pay for a midwife to help me to deliver the baby at a clinic. So when I went to the clinic to give birth my contractions were normal but I had complications during the birthing process. My baby had turned sideways. The midwife called the doctor to help her and he came right away. He said there was no time to give me medicine for my pain and I had to deliver the baby naturally. The doctor used his hand to turn the baby and some forceps to pull the baby by the head to get the baby to come down through the pelvic. But she wouldn't turn. It was a miracle that she lived because my umbilical cord was around her neck and there was no time to call for an ambulance to take me to the emergency room. He had to do what he did because she could have suffocated and died.

After they cleaned my baby up I was laying on the bed waiting to see my baby. When I started hemorrhaging. I felt blood gushing out of my womb and when the nurse came back into the room and saw me laying in a puddle of blood, she said oh Lord she is hemorrhaging. Then another nurse came running in the room and began to apply pressure to my abdomen. God gave me two miracles that day not only did he save my baby life but he also spared my life again.   Lord I thank you!!

Miracle Healing for Emotional Trauma

I had been praying and fasting for three days for my family, friends, pastor and the lost. On the third day I was on my knees on the side of my bed and I went to get up when I heard the voice of the Lord say you have prayed for everybody else now I want you to pray for you. I want to heal the wounds of your heart. I said Lord I'm ok. Then a vision of me pop up when I was a little girl. I jump up and ran into the restroom saying Lord please don't open the door of my past abuse and rejection from my family, it still hurt so bad. I heard Him say no one can hurt you like that again. I want to heal you so the devil can't use it to hurt you anymore. I cried as God played each event before my eyes like I was watching a movie video. I saw myself as a child and each person that hurt me. I heard the Lord say forgive them they can't hurt you no more. I looked at each one of them as a child and said why did you hurt me or hate me. In the video they didn't say anything then I would say to each one I forgive you. When the Lord had finished playing the video

He said I am going to stitch your heart so that the wounds are never open again. God said after today it won't ever hurt the same. It is 2013 and God has been faithful, my life has never been the same. Thank You Jesus I love you.

The Angel Made My Path Straight Miracle

I was late on my rent not because I didn't have the money. I had my rent in a money order on the first but bad weather prevented me from driving across town to take it to the landlord. I normally paid my rent on the first day of the month but because of a severe storm and continual rain for two none stop days I couldn't. The News Media were telling everyone that the city was flooded and to stay in because all the roads were underwater. My neighborhood was totally underwater. On the third day during the late afternoon the water began to reseed from my neighborhood and I took the rent to the landlord who lived on the other side of the city. There was still a lot of water around the city but I made it to her and when I knocked on the door to give her the rent she said she wanted late fees. I explained to her that I paid my rent on the first normally. I realized it was not the 1st but it's was the third of the month and that we just had a storm for two days with raining and flooding, that I could not get the payment to her. Then she said I don't want the rent without the late charges. I was on a real tight budget and I did not have extra money. I said ok and I turned around and went home. The next week she filed for my eviction in the court. Well I had to go to court and I was so sick on the day of court with the flu that I could hardly get out of bed. I had a very high fever and my body ached all over and my voice was totally gone. I prayed and said Lord I am so sick I don't feel like talking, my head hurt, my body hurt, Lord please help me. I heard the Lord say to me I will be your attorney, your judge and your jury. I got up put my clothes on and went to court. When the judge called my eviction case I got up to answer his question and the landlord got up too. The judge ask why was I late. I said because of the storm situation. He said I remember that, he asked the landlord why didn't she take the rent. She said she was late plus I am pregnant and I don't have insurance so I need the money. She said she owe me late fees and rent. The judge asked me if I had the rent and I said yes. The judge asked the landlord do you want the rent and she said no. He asked me if he could see the money order and I showed it to him it had the first day of the month. And Judge said the first is on it. She said I want the rent and my house. The judge said you can have either the rent or the house but you will not get both. He said most people would be happy to get their rent what is wrong with you? The Judge said this make no sense. He asked her again do you want your rent. She said no my house. He said ok Julie you have the rest of the month to find you a place to lived and don't give her the rent used it for your rent at your next place. He said you have seven days left in the month. I said thank you. I needed a miracle. I didn't have a car so I didn't have a way around to look for a place. I had my step sister to take me around and look for a place when she could the rest of time I looked in the Newspaper and made calls to check on places. I had four days left and I had not found a place to live.

I sat down at my dinette table and prayed while I eat then went in the kitchen. I was standing in front of the refrigerator door and I looked straight ahead and there appear an angel with wings white as snow, hair was auburn (reddish) and I notice the detail of the hair. The angel didn't have one string of hair out of place. I said Lord how beautiful are the works of your hands. The angel just glided no gravity. Then as the angel got closer I heard the Lord say watch but don't touch and I did what I was told. I watch the angel glide or flowed straight by me, the angel never looked to the right or to the left. Only glided straight through the wall and disappeared. After the angel left I heard the spirit of the Lord say now go and look in the green sheet ad. I did. I looked down in the house rental section and this house magnified itself in bold letter and pop off the page. I said lord this is more than I'm paying now I can't afford this. I called my stepsister and asked her if she could take me to this address because I did not have any ideal where it was. She took me and the house was only a few blocks in the same community from where I lived. It was a two story brick home that had recently been renovated. My son and daughters got out the car and ran to the backyard then they came running back to the front saying mama this is our house. The lord used them as my confirmation but I didn't realize it. So I told them to get in the car because they were so loud with joy the neighbors could hear them. They were so happy. I had already packed up all boxes. I called the management company and the lady came out and showed me the house and we talked for two hours about her life and my situation and from where I was moving from. At the end of our conversation she said when do you want to move. I said when can I move I need to be out by Friday and it was Wednesday. She asked me what color carpet did I want in the house and I picked out the carpet The Property Manager said I can come by your house tomorrow and bring the keys and I can get the rent from you and you can start moving in. They should be finish with the carpet by tomorrow evening. She did and I started moving in on Thursday evening. God is so good. Oh how I love Him, He is always on time

Created Miracles

I was looking for a new job in the city I was living in before God moved me out of the city. I had a job already that I got paid every two weeks. I had applied for a clerical job at the courthouse in the city and they had called me for an interview and a typing test. On the job I was working my wage was very low so I was living on a very tight budget. There wasn't much income for nothing else once I paid my bills and bought grocery from the store. And if something unexpected came up I was primarily in a bad situation. This was one of those days that I didn't have money and I didn't have enough gas to get to my clerical interview so I drove to several of my family members in the neighborhood and asked them for five dollar until Friday, it was midweek. My interview was only about five miles away. And nobody I asked had five dollars to spared until Friday. (now you know that was bad nobody had even five dollars to spare) I prayed for a miracle in my gas tank that I would make it to the interview and back. I refused to look at the dashboard at my gas needle in order to keep my faith. I made it to my interview and took my typing test and it was time to go home. I got in my car and prayed again but I refused to look at the gas needle. When I made it in the driveway of my home I said thank you Lord than I looked down at my gas needle and it showed it was full. I thought the gas was so low in the tank it must have gotten air in it and the air must have pushed my needle to full. God granted me a miracle but I could not believe. I ask forgiveness right now as I look back on how good God has been to me. So on Friday I drove down the street to work. After I got paid I went to the gas station to fill up my car and as I turned the gas cap I was expecting to hear the releasing of air pressure coming from the tank but I didn't. I place the gas hose into the gas tank and press it and gas rush back out of the tank so I was still thinking it was full of air so I put the gas hose back in the tank and squeezed the hose very slowly and gas still came out running down the side of my car. I begin laughing and say my God had filled up my car with gas how awesome was that. Then I really understood the scripture which said the just must live by faith and although I was surprise He still grant it to me at end of the day. I had only trusted Him to get me to my interview and home and He did it anyway for me. My God had done abundantly above what I could ask that day. Our God help in the time of need and trouble. Thank you Jesus!

Miracle Payment of Bill

I paid my light bill by check and it bounced because I didn't have the money in the bank account. And after they added the overdraft fee for the bank and for the light company I really didn't have it. I prayed that the light company wouldn't come out until Friday to turn off the lights cause by then I would have the payment and late fees. During this time if you had the money when they came to the door you could pay them on the spot and they wouldn't turn your lights off. The light company came out that Thursday evening to turn the light off. I thought oh no Lord I won't have the money until tomorrow, Lord help, my children are going to be in the dark. Lord I don't have nobody I can ask for the money. I went to the door and spoke with the gentleman from the utility company who had come out to turn the lights off after he knocked on the door. He said I came to turn your lights off. I said I paid the bill and I have a receipt for it. My hope was that the bank covered it and I would have to pay over draft fees. He looked at me and said hold on I don't know why they sent me out here because even on my document says its paid.

Now this is awesome the gentlemen said it showed paid on the document. Then he said I need to go and radio the company about your bill I'll be right back. I said ok and while he was gone I prayed again. He came back and said ma'am I'm sorry the company told me to leave them on because your bill is paid. God paid it for me. Hallelujah! The money for the bill was never pulled from my account and the next month I only got a bill which confirm God handle it. The previous bill was not added. God paid my bill. God will make a way when there seem to be no way.

<u>Miracle Garment</u>

I had an engagement for ministry and had a two piece outfit made with a matching hat for my licensing and ordination service. I had prayed and asked God what color to wear and He told me white So I asked my stepsister to come and get me and take me to the fabric store because I didn't have transportation to get there. Soon as I got in the fabric store my stepsister begin rushing me. She kept saying hurry up. I told her if she couldn't bring me to the store she should have told me before she brought me. So I asked a worker in the store if she could help me and I told her what I was looking for. The worker pulled the fabric for me and I told her how much I needed. The fabric was double on the roll so looking at it I couldn't tell how thick it was until later. I took it to the seamstress and she looked at it but didn't say nothing about the fabric either. I really didn't know that much about fabric at the time. So I thought everything was good. Than two days before my licensing I was trying to call someone else when out of nowhere my phone dialed the seamstress phone number. I didn't even know her number by heart and this was strange. During the time I did not have a cell phone. When the seamstress answered the phone I asked for the person I was calling, then I recognized her voice and she said Julie. I said yes I'm sorry I wasn't trying to call you. She said I'm glad you called the material you brought me is for a blouse and it's too thin for a skirt. I said why didn't you call and tell me. She didn't say nothing. I said have you finished making the dress, she said no. I said can you finish it by tomorrow. She said yes. I told her to just continue because I don't have a choice but to wear it now. So I hung up and prayed Lord I don't have no money to buy another dress, I need your help. Tell me what to do, the seamstress is saying the fabric is too thin for a dress, that it's only suitable for a blouse. It's not like God didn't hear my conversation with her. But He didn't say anything. So I went to the store and bought a slip, the button and ribbon for the blouse, skirt and hat. When I took the stuff to the seamstress and she finished the outfit it was too short, it was above my knees. I was so upset about the length. I said Lord you know I don't wear my clothes above my knees but I don't have a choice. So I took the outfit home and laid hands on it and prayed over it and put it in the closet. But it bothered me all evening and all night. The next day I got dress for my ordination service the skit was lengthen way below my knees like I like it. God had given me a miracle on the length of my skirt. After I was ordained and licensed I got so many compliments about my outfit. No one knew it was the wrong material. it was thicker than it originally looked. This just blew me away there is no words I can say about what God did for me other than Wow He Is Amazing!!

Miracle After Giving An Offering

I didn't have a job I was a stay home mom and my budget was very little money at the time. After my child support check I paid my tithes and offering than my bills, sometime all I had was three dollars left to my name. Than one day I had three dollars and the spirit of the Lord said send the three dollars to Copeland Ministry. I did, it was my last three dollars, I didn't even have the money to put it in a money order. I just put it in a stamped envelope between some tablet paper which I had put my name, address, the amount I was sending and put it in the community mail box to mail off. I said ok Lord that was all I had and I went about during my daily house task. About two hour later my husband came home and said here is three hundred dollars in a money order that I have been intending to give you but I keep forgetting to give it to you. My obedience in doing what God said cause him to bring to my husband mind about the money he had forgot to give me. He gave it to me and I said thank you Lord. Then my next instruction was given the Lord said put it up. So I did as I was told. Weeks went by and then months. Then one evening I heard the Lord say call the radio station and get on the air. I said ok. Then I said to myself what will I be saying on the radio. I called the station and spoke with manager about a spot on the air. She said she would like to meet with me but where she wanted to meet with me was about an hour from where I lived. Meeting the manager there was close than going to the station to meet her. I said Lord how am I to get there I still had no car. The Lord totally instructed me in what to do. He said catch a ride to your mom with your husband then a friend of our family was at my mother house who took me to the Restaurant for the meeting. He took me to meeting and dropped me off. When I was exiting the car he asked me if I wanted him to come back and get me. I said do you mine, he said no, he was so happy to do it. I went in and met with the radio manager from the radio station. We talked about all the fees, the different times she had available and I sign a contract with her. Right after I sign the contract the friend came in and said are you ready? He took me back to my mom house. When I got there my uncle was there, he lived near me. When I walked through the door he spoke to me and said he was about to go home. I said uncle can I get a ride home. He said yes you sure can are you ready to go. I said yes and he took me home. Lord I thank you. When I got home I begin to think Lord what am I going to say on the radio and more than that how am I going to pay the bill every two weeks. I heard God say I don't want you to ask for money on the radio I want you to trust me. I was on the air live Monday thru Friday for fifteen minutes. And at first it seemed like the longest fifteen minutes of my life. People began calling me after the broadcast and God would use me to minister to them and I can say God did not let one of my words fall to the ground. Than people started calling in telling their testimony. And after the broadcast I would be praying for people for hours. My Jesus is so awesome, He bless His people and He paid the bill every two weeks and I didn't miss not one payment.

Obedience Is Important and God Gave Me Miracle

I needed a car I had been without a car for a long time almost a year, I actually think it was going on ten months. I bought a car from a second chance program and I had the money to pay the payment but I held on to it so I wouldn't be without money until my next pay day. Obedient is better than sacrifice. I had held the money in my purse for ten days. The morning of the tenth day I heard the Spirit of Lord say pay your car payment. I thought in my mind I'm only ten days late, they probably have a late fee I'll pay it. That evening I heard the Spirit of the Lord say put your car in the garage and I was going to do it after I finish dishes. Then about thirty minutes later I heard the Lord say again put your car in the garage so I call my son and told him to put my car in the garage. He said ok I'll do it in just a few minutes. About fifteen minutes later someone rang the doorbell and it was the repo man and he said I came to pick up your car. I said I have the money right here I just didn't have time to go and pay it. I said I will go and pay it in the morning. He hooked up my car to his wrecker and drove off. I was so hurt and mad at the same time because I didn't obey the Spirit of the Lord and I let fear of being without money until my next paycheck. I was not obedient three times one by not paying the car payment when He told me and twice by not putting my car in the garage. I walk along time for not obeying. I let worry and anxiety get in my way. God was teaching me to trust Him and obey His voice and I had a costly lesson. I cried out Lord I had the money to pay the car payment I'm so sorry for not obeying you. I will not do it again. Then I heard Him say the enemy wont gloat over you. I didn't understand what He meant nor did I know that I would be ten months without a vehicle.

My instruction was to prepare for time alone with God. Then the Lord told me that I want you to shut the door to everybody and everything for a season and read the entire bible, I want to teach you. He told me there would be no girly hanging out time. He wanted me to go to church and back home in my bible. He told me to get some tablets and write down what I learn. Even the more I begin to understand the Holy Spirit purpose and He taught me so much during this time and answered so many question that I had.

Sanctify Time with The Lord

One evening while I was walking for exercise and praying to God I heard the Lord say after you finish reading the bible I going to give you a car and I said ok Lord and I believed Him. About two months before I finished reading the bible I heard a horn blow in my garage. I ran to the garage and looked in there and no car so I went and looked out the living room window and there was nobody out side. I said Lord I know I heard a horn blow. He didn't say nothing. Then again about a month before I finished reading the bible I heard the horn blow again in the garage and it was the exact horn that I heard the month before blowing the same way, with two quick horn sound. Again I ran to the garage door and peaked into the garage and nobody was there so I ran to the front room and looked out the window to catch who ever blew the horn but when I got there no one was outside. I said Lord I know I heard a horn but He didn't say nothing. When I finished reading the bible the Lord told me to go to a specific dealership and look at a car. I only knew where one was and it was out of town so I went and I was turned down. As I was driving back home disappointed I said Lord I know you told me to go there. And He didn't say nothing. The next day I went into the garage and I cleaned it out and I told my husband and children do not put anything on this side of the garage because this is where my new car is going. My husband laugh and said ok. He looked like right, sure you getting a new car. About 1 week later I was coming from church with a friend and I saw a sign saying that specific dealership was in my city. I asked my friend can you take me over there and she did but I didn't really look because it was dark. But I had found the other dealership, it was a lesson to me on how important it is to be at the right place. See I had testified in church that God was going to give me a new car to those who knew my situation and they just look at me with unbelief but I testify anyway. Weeks passed. I asked my husband if I could use his company truck which was a big Chevrolet. I drove back to the car lot with my bible and my faith stirred up because I knew what God had promised me. He would give me a new car when I finished reading the bible. It was already the tenth month. When I made it to the car lot I set there and prayed with my bible closed on the seat. After I finished praying I went to open the door to get out of the truck when all of sudden I notice my bible open itself and the pages began to turned like the wind was blowing in the truck and I looked and both of my windows were up. When I looked down at the pages turning then stopped in the first chapter of the book of Joshua and verse nine magnified itself as if it lifted itself off the page. Then I read it and it said, Have I not commanded you to be strong and of good courage, do not be afraid nor be dismayed for I the Lord your God is with you wherever you go. The car lot was closed so I looked around and I began praying and praising God on the lot. I begin lifting my hands and dancing around and next thing I knew a security guard was walking over to me saying you alright. I said yes I'm just praising the Lord for what He has done for me. While I was still praying he turn and left and went back to where ever he came from. Two weeks later early on a Saturday morning I was lying in bed thinking when I heard the Spirit of God say get ready it's time to go.

God's Appointed Time for A Miracle

I jump up and started putting on my clothes and I thought to myself where am I going with no car. Then I said Lord where am I going. He said to get your car. I continue to get dress. You see every time the lord spoke joy took me over. I then thought how will I get there. Then I said Lord how will I get there. The Father said call your brother. I picked up the phone and called my brother and he said yes he would take me but it would be later so I said ok and hung up. After I hung up I thought call my mother and she said she would take me and was on her way. Then she called me backed and said she couldn't come. I said ok and hung up the phone with her. Then I was thinking who else could I call. About ten minute later my brother called back and said I'm on my way I can't go back to sleep. See the lord visited him. While I was waiting on him to come I was thinking what kind of car was I to get. I knew exactly what lot I was going to but I didn't have an ideal what car I was getting and God didn't tell me either. It wasn't long before my brother made it to my house and he stop by a garage sale and bought me a brand new dress that still had the price tag on it and it was my size too. Me and my kids loaded up in my brother car and we head to the car lot. Then my brother said do you have your down payment for your new car, I said yeah I have everything I need. He didn't know that all I had was a promise from God and the faith that He would do it, that was it. When we made it to the car lot they were having a major sale. They had balloons everywhere, popcorn, hotdogs and sodas, it was like God threw a party just for me. My brother said you want me to wait on you. I said I don't need you to, we're going to drive home. There were sales people everywhere, when we dove up I saw this one sales person in one of the carts driving to the back of the lot. I said Lord who going to help me and he said him. I said Lord he is going the other way across the parking lot. By the time I got out of the car he was gone. Me and the kids got out the car and started walking to go in the building and when we grab the door the guy which was in the cart met me as I open the door and he said how can I help you'll today. I was actually startle because I didn't see him. I said I came to buy a car but I didn't know which one. He said okay how is your credit score. I said good. He said okay how much money are you putting down. I said I don't know, but I need you to work for me, can you do that for me. I said I need you to do exactly what I tell you to do, can you do that. He said yes. I said I first need you to go and pull my credit score and come back then I will know what kind of down payment I will have, he said ok and he did exactly what I asked him to do. He was nice about doing it. He came back and said you can get a car for 14,999.00. I said okay can you point me in that direction where the cars cost this amount and he did. I went to look at the cars and while I was looking at these two car the sales person can back so quickly and said you found it. I tried to move my feet and couldn't, all I could move was the upper part of my body.

My Feet Were Order by The Lord

Then I look at the car I was standing by and said yeah this one because the color of it. He walked around and looked at the price on the window and said it's the right price. He said let me get the keys so you can test drive. What I didn't know is it was a standard shift Toyota. I had never driven a stick shift. My son learned how to drive a standard by riding on a lawn mower. I was able to test drive it on the parking lot. When we got back he said what kind of down payment do you have. I said can you get my paper and when he left I prayed and I heard the Lord say give him a thousand dollars check. When he came back I gave him the check then he took me in the finance office. While I was sitting there the finance officer computer screen start rolling like a Television tube was getting ready to blow out. It kept rolling and the finance person was hitting his computer keyboard trying to stop it. I begin to stand and say something to help him when I heard the Lord said be quite, I am giving you a miracle. So I sat back down and was silent. The sale person gave me some forms to fill out which I did. Then he said you need insurance. The salesperson knew someone who sold insurance that was on call. I needed two hundred and thirty dollars and all I had was one hundred ninety dollars so my son gave me the rest. We got the insurance and my sixteen years old son drove us home. When we got home I got out the car to open the garage and I told my son to hit the horn and it was the exact horn I heard several months earlier. Now I knew God was saying to me it was on the way each time I heard the horn blow. I bought a car I couldn't really drive. I ask the Holy Spirit what to do and He taught me how to drive a standard shift. He taught me when to lift my feet off the clutch and give it gas. He taught me when to shift from first, second, third, fourth and fifth gear and then how to down shift. He taught me how to hold the clutch and gas when sitting on an incline. I learned that the Holy Spirit was not only a teacher of spiritual thing but of natural things. The Auto company send me a thank you letter for purchasing your new car. They never cash the thousand dollars check and I never had to pay a dime for the car. God gave me a brand new car with three miles on it. there is nobody like my GOD.   Miracles still happens.

Ministry Building and Favor

I was doing house to house Bible Studies and the Father later told me to start a radio ministry and which station to go on which I did. I enjoy my time with the Lord with my daily bible reading, personal study, pray, fasting and worship. I found joy in God's presence and doing the radio ministry was not something I desire. I was so enjoying the presence of the Lord and the Holy Spirit teaching me the meat of the scriptures. I set a time to meet with the lord every day and I schedule my schedule so I would not miss my time in His presence we meet every day at the same time, same place and I really looked forward to our time alone. One day while in the presence of the Lord in our meeting time the Lord said I want you to go and find a building to start doing ministry. I said ok. It was right after the Lord gave me my miracle car. He said we won't meet this way after you start the radio broadcast but we will always be together. I did not like the change from being in the presence of the lord every day at the same time. When I look back over it, it was not the schedule but the growing up and doing ministry. People are difficult some time and you can never please them. God was different all you have to do is obey Him. He assured me we would always be together but thing would be just at a little different. I went out and found a building. I didn't have no money as usual to get a building. I didn't have money even for the first month rent. I went back home and prayed about the building I found. The Lord said call them to see the inside of the building. I did and when I met the owner we talked and afterward he asked me when would I like to start. I heard the Lord say the fifteenth so I said the fifteenth of August. The building was 1,200 square feet and he wanted seven hundred dollars a month all utilities paid. It was beautiful, blue title floor and Blinds with large windows two entry doors, air condition, office, class room, seated 50-75 people. So the owner said all I need is a check and we can get started. I said ok but you can't cash the check until the thirty-first of August. I explained I need the keys today so I can be ready by the fifteenth. He said ok and gave me the keys. This was around the fifth or the sixth of August. As I mention earlier I was doing house ministry rotating from one house to next each week. So when I got the building I went to them and told them that I had just got a building. They were eager to help with what I needed. They bought the chairs and tables, curtains, all the children supply, filing cabinet, my office desk, micro wave, telephone with an answer machine, keyboard, speakers, stereo player for our media room, and on the fifteenth I was able to open the doors for ministry. Our media room was a closet which we cut a small window so the media person could communicate with me. It was awesome the guys would literally rush to church to run the media room.

Our keyboard was a small keyboard with speaker from radio shack for volume. We didn't have a pulpit or podium and no money to buy one. The Lord told me to go to the new construction site where they were building new home in the neighborhood and ask for the wood they were throwing away and I did and they told me I could get all the wood I needed. Me and a little mother who was sixty-eight years old in the church packed it to my house in my miracle car. I let the back window down and put as much as I could put on the seat and open my trunk and filled it and when I got home I realize I didn't know anybody who could build a podium. So I prayed Lord who going to build the podium and He said go ask the man across the street. So I went across the street and knocked on the door. A gentleman came to the door, I said Sir do you do carpenter work. He said yes. I said do you know how to build a church podium with a book holder like this one in this book. He just smiled and said bring me some wood and we'll see what I can do. So I told him I have some in my garage that I got from the home builder down the street that they gave me. I took it to him, he looked at it and said old yeah, I can build it out of this and he did. He stain the wood and charge me one hundred dollars for making it. Now the church was complete and I had a professional looking pulpit and podium. I was ready to open the church. We started with twenty members and visitors. I had announced also on the radio that I was opening a ministry building and people begin coming from the radio broadcast. I was having worship service twice on Sunday, eleven o'clock and seven o'clock in the evening and Wednesday at seven o'clock in the evening. God would show up every service and every service were packed out. Now this was funny when I look back. I invited a professional piano player to come and play for us. He came to play and when he looked at my piano he said is this it. I said yep. It was our one hundred and fifty dollar piano and stand from radio shack. He got on it and played it like he was playing a Yamaha Motif. It was rocking back and forth like it was dancing with the beat. It was a miracle it didn't burn up because he had it smoking and we had some church that day. God was using me in the prophetic and healing ministry. People with every kind of sickness and disease were being heal the whole time in that building. People were healed of Aids, cancer, leukemia, depression, witchcraft spells, and I even seen the dead raised. God took away smokers desire to smoke, heart disease, high blood just to name a few things He did. We also began to do outreach by going door to door praying for people. We started feeding people during the holidays. And God bless me and the people of the church in that twelve hundred square feet building. I didn't despise my small beginning.

<u>Miracle Provision</u>
Ministry and Home

I was short on my rent payment, my husband and I had a small group of people. We were not in full time ministry meaning getting paid from ministry. We did not have enough money to pay the ministry rent and our home rent. My husband work as a manager for a company. Most of our income went within ministry. We had been faithful in taking care of the things of God when it came to paying the ministry payment. Now we were in need of seven hundred dollars for our rent. So my husband and I prayed for a miracle and I heard the Lord say go to the bank before midnight and pull it from your bank account. It was around thirty minutes before midnight so my husband and I jumped in our vehicle and rush to the bank. I stuck the debit card in the bank money machine, put in our pin number, typed the amount we needed and seven hundred dollars came out. We knew our bank balance was zero because we had gone earlier and pull all the money we had out in. We kept checking to see if we would get an overdraft letter or if our account would be noted for it but it never did. My husband kept thinking maybe they were going to take if from his direct deposit but it wasn't. The next month God met us again the same way with the same exact amount. We praise God for doing the impossible in our life. Not only did He do it once but He confirm it was Him and He did it a second time. God was supplying our needs at this time not our wants. I heard God say he don't always come the same way. I am thankful he showed up. What a good loving Father we have in God.

Miracle Transportation and Favor

My husband truck was repossessed because he was using his vehicle payment to make the ministry payment because our membership had dropped and we were short on rent. My husband began riding the bus to work and he had just found a second job and needed transportation to get there. I was using a friend's vehicle I was driving down one of the main street in our city on my way home. They had several car lots on this main street. The angel of the Lord took my steering wheel and turn it to the right into a car lot which was closed. The Lord said go look in the window of the garage where they clean cars. I went and looked in the window and it was the make ready area and there was a green corolla there. So I left and on Monday morning I went and talked to a salesman about the car. He ran my credit and said I was approved and all I needed was a thousand dollars to put down. I didn't have a dime. I told the salesman wait a minute I needed to step outside. I went and prayed and God told me to write the check and I did. I don't know what happen to that check because it never made it to my bank nor did I ever hear anything else about it. I just know that I didn't have a dime in our account. All I know is God took care of it no matter what happen to it. Thank you Jesus!

Rise The Die Miracle

A little mother in the church sister was in the hospital sick and we had been praying for her. On this day I received a phone call from the little mother saying her sister heart had stop beating and had just pass away and the doctor pronounce her dead. I heard the Spirit of the Lord say it was not her time and I was to pray her back to life. I had never prayed for anyone who pass away before. I asked the little mother if she would go back in the hospital room because the Lord said that it was not time for her baby sister to die. I asked if she had any anointing oil and if she would put some on her finger and place it on her sister heart. She said yes. I told her I was going to be praying until I heard back from her. I did and the sister can back to life. The little mother was so happy. Her sister told the family the story of dying and seeing her love one and they told her to go back it was not time. What I learned here is sometime people prematurely die but if we ask God if it was their time, if it's not pray and call them back in their body, God is able to do the impossible.

Healing A Patient Miracle

One afternoon my uncle's wife called to tell me her sister was in the hospital. She explained her sister need a match for bone marrow transplant. The doctor tested the entire family and there was no match. My aunt's sister would go in and out of comas frequently. It got worst and my aunt kept saying she not going to make. I got so angry at the devil. I tried to be an encourager. I said God is able to do what no man can. I will stand in the gap for her with you. My aunt would call me and tell me what the report was on her sister. She had cancer and lupus a blood disease. One day on a Saturday I receive a call from my aunt and she said we are standing in the hall of the hospital and the doctor said my sister will not make it after today, she is in a coma. I said I still believe God is able to do the impossible. After I hung up the telephone with my aunt I heard the Lord say its time, go now to the hospital. I didn't have a car so I call one of the members of the church I attended and I ask if she could give me a ride to the hospital. She said yes, she picked me up and drove me to the hospital. When I got there the family was still standing in the hall just like my aunt told me. I said may I go in to see her, the family said yes. I put on scrub and a mask to protect her immune system. When I enter the room the young lady opened her eyes. I ask her if I could pray for her? She said sure you can but before you do can I tell you something. I said yes. She said I had a dream that there was a wolf and he jump at me with his teeth showing ready to bite me next a glass fell down between us. I interpreted her dream. I explain it as the spirit of the Lord gave it to me. I said the wolf was the devil who can to destroy you and the glass represented Jesus the Christ who stood between you and the wolf to protect you. She said oh! I then explained to her that I was going to take just my little pinky and lay it on top of her hand and I would pray if that was okay. (Now this was the instruction I receive from the Holy Spirit.) She said yes ma'am that will be fine. I prayed for her and thank her for letting me pray for her and she said no thank you. The lady had children who need her. I left believing God that she was heal. On that following Monday they gave her chemo and it burned her feet and hands. So they ran test to see what was going on and could not find any lupus or cancer in her body. She called me. She told me that the doctors couldn't find the lupus or the cancer and she wanted to know what did I think she should do. I ask her did she believe that God had heal her and she said yes. I said it really up to you what you decide to do. She said I am going home to my family and trust God. She said I've lost a lot a weight but I am going home. As of today she is still alive and well. Glory to God the Most High. Glory!!!

Chapter 5

VISIONS & DREAMS WARNING OF DANGER

I was approximately age four and half when I had a dream that my brothers and one of my sisters died. When I awoke I did not know that it was a dream. I ran to my parents and told them that I saw my brother and sister die. I was screaming that it was a snake bite that caused their deaths. My father took me by my arms forcefully to shake me and told me to never say that again. I felt like I had done wrong. I did not understand why he was so angry. One morning the following week after my dad had left for work my mother left right after him with her friends to go to the club. It was that day that I was imitating my mother by trying to clean the house (as I seen my mom always do) I took the furniture polish from under the kitchen cabinet and put it on the coffee table to polish the furniture in the living room. I walk away from the table to clean something and when I looked back I saw my brother drinking from the polish top and my sister that was 18 months old drinking from the bottle. I ran to take it from her but it was too late, she had ingested it. I was home all day with her and my sibling alone. We were locked in I couldn't reach the latch to go for help. I stood at a window looking for anyone to walk by to ask for help but there was no one for hours. I remember my sister screaming and crying. I was unable to help her I didn't know what to do. When my parents came home they rushed her to the hospital but it was too late, she died holding on to my dad's thumb. I found out years later God warned them through other but no one heeded.

<u>Vision of Jesus Christ</u>

I was walking around my house and God kept giving me a vision of the cross for three days. I kept saying Lord I don't understand, what are you saying, am I to preach or teach on the cross. Then on the third day He showed me the cross again but this time I saw myself standing beside the cross. Then I saw myself spiritually walking away from my physically me that was standing beside the cross. It was as if I was leaving the old me but I still didn't understand. Then my spiritual man looked back and told my physical man that it couldn't go where I was going spiritually. I felt afraid because I knew the old me but I wasn't sure where God was taking the new me. My spirit man kept walking away from my old man only to leave me beside the cross. The new me or the spirit me heard the voice of God say get in the blood. I looked down and there was a lake of blood in front of me. I said Jesus I am afraid, will you go with me. Then all of a sudden Jesus appeared in the blood. I got in his arms and He held me like a baby and submerged me in the blood. When He came up with me He said these word, there will be times when you don't feel saved, but when those time come remember this day. I did not understand it then. But I went through a period like no other in my life. Lead in the wilderness by the Lord with manifold trials. It was then that I understand the word the Lord spoke. I am grateful for His mercy and His grace. Jesus I Love You

Heavenly Visitation

I got filled with the Holy Spirit one night at church. After leaving church that night I went home and praised God for filling me with the Precious Holy Spirit. While standing in my kitchen I was lead to look at the clock it read 12 mid night. I began to thank God for saving me and filling me with His Holy Spirit. I don't remember what all happen but I was taken to heaven and found myself on my knees before the Father and Jesus. I always questioned why we need to pray to the Father in Jesus name. The Father was sitting on the throne beside Jesus so I was talking to him though I could not see his face. I kept talking to Him asking for forgiveness for the world's sin. He never answered but Jesus did. I ask Jesus why when I talk to Him you answer. Jesus explain I and the Father are one and no one can speak to the Father accept they go through Me. I ask Jesus, how is it that you know what he wants to say? He said they were of the same mind and on one accord so whatever I want to say to the Father I need to say to him. I then turned and asked Jesus to tell the Father to forgive us on earth. After I had finish praying and talking to Jesus I immediately felt the presence of someone coming. I look toward the door and seen this tall angel come in. I ask Jesus what was it that he wanted. Jesus said to me ask him. I never open my mouth but the angel said it is time to go back. I learned something in heaven, they didn't talk like we do, it was more of what was said in thought (Proverbs 23:7for as he thinketh in his heart, so is he.) I realize then that Jesus only answers for the Father. When I return I was standing in my living room by the window. I was lead to look at the clock it was 6 am in the morning. I look out the window and realized I had been in the presence of God all night and it seemed as if it had only been 15 minutes. There is no time in eternality. That same day a miracle happened. I went to one my sister's house that was on drugs at the time and knock on her door to pray with her but she was not home. I had a salvation track and was lead to put it in the door. When I stuck it in her door it was if someone on the other side pulled it from my hand. I later ask my sister did she get the salvation track I left. She said yes they were all over my floor in my house from my living room, down the hall and into my bed room. How did you get in? I told her I didn't go in her house. I began to explain that I only had one and put it in her door. She is off drugs today Glory to God for His loving kindness.

<u>Vision the Father Speaks</u>

I was praising God one morning and was caught up in the Spirit. I saw Jesus on the throne and I came in and kneeled before Him and said my mission is complete. As I stood up, in my hand was a big jewel with many people in it of all races and nationalities. For the first time I heard the voice of the Father. The Father said the only thing you could ever give Jesus is souls. This is why he came to earth and died. I took the jewel and placed it in the crown of Jesus. I looked and there were places on his crown for more jewels to be placed. I then heard the Father say never let them (people of God) forget the only thing they could ever give Him (Jesus) is souls (Revelation 5:12-14).

Appearance of Jesus

While hosting a three days conference, that I entitled Recitation Conference in the Dallas, Texas. Healing and deliverance took place. Jesus appeared in the Church with a message. Saying not much time left before His Return for His Bride. There was a measurement tape or ruler used for illustration of the time left. Jesus enter the church door dress in a Gold Robe with scarlet red trim. I shared it with church that Jesus had just walk in and what I seen that night. People left that meeting healed, changed and delivered. That very night marriages were restored, businesses came forth, the churches were resituated and the Body of Christ were revived. Joy returned to the House of God that night. And I heard that the people have been growing in their faith and walking in the Love of Christ. It blesses me to see the broken hearts heal. One young man came up and said to me you have a ministry that heals the broken hearted. He experience healing emotionally. He explained that he had been suicidal after breaking up with his wife and never being able to see his new born child. The lord allowed me to speak a word of encouragement and the words were fulfilled. His family came home. God care for us and desires healing and wholeness in our lives.

Angel Provide Guidance

I move to Houston, Texas. I didn't want to move away from my family but I had a dream. I told my mother about my dream to move to Houston. She didn't want me to move away. It was only an hour drive away. My mother said I will help you pay rent if you need me to just don't move to Houston, Texas. I tried to stay there to be with family but everywhere I went the doors were closed. Everywhere I placed my application either someone was approved that day or we found out the house was already leased. I said okay Lord I give up. I realized the Lord had closed the doors in that city and was not going to move on my behalf until I relocated. I ask my step sister who lived in Houston to help me look since she was from the city of Houston, Texas. She did but nothing was opening up to me. I ask her to send me the applications she had for me and when she did I notice she had told many lies on the applications. I understood she thought she was helping me out in order for me to get approved. I explained to her that I couldn't lie either God is with me or He is not. In my dreams God gave me street names and the cross road. So I started looking for a home in that area and drove to Houston myself. I spoke with a lady over the phone concerning her rental house. It was a nice brick home. I went to see her at a dry cleaner business she owned. I ask her what she needed from me to rent this home. When I spoke with the owner she said just give me the deposit and the rent, I didn't even have to fill out an application. I was messed up. I ask how much for rent? She told me and then she asked if I had it with me? I said yes. She then said you want to move when? I replied, soon as possible. She said here are the keys, just get a money order and make it out to me. She said I need to clean the house but have not gotten around to it yet. She was pregnant and had just purchased a new home. I told her I would clean it if that would be okay with her? She said yes. It was the very location I saw in the dream. The very street and cross street God gave me in the dream, God made sure I didn't

miss it. God gave me a miracle and made sure the bills and rent were paid every month. Thank you Lord you are so awesome

Scriptures

No man hath seen God at any time; the only begotten Son, which is in the bosom of the Father, he hath declared him. John 1:18

Many have seen Christ

Jesus was seen after His resurrection
1Corinthians 15:1-11

12 different recorded appearances of Jesus:
1st of 12 The appearance of Jesus to Marry Magdalene Sunday 17th or 21st of Nisan Matthew 28:1, Mark 16:9-11, John 20:11-18

2nd of 12 The appearance of Jesus to the other women Matthew 28:1

3rd of 12 The appearance of Jesus to two disciples (Cleophas and another) on the road to Emmaus Mark 16:12-13, Luke 24:13-32, John 24:33-35, 1 Corinthians 15:5

4th of 12 The news of the appearance of Jesus to Simon Peter Luke 24:33-35, 1 Corinthians 15:5

5th of 12 The appearance to the astonished disciples (Thomas absent) with a commission Mark 16:14, Luke 24:36-43, 1 Corinthians 15:5

6th of 12 The appearance of Jesus to the disciples the next Sunday night John 20:26-31

7th of 12 The appearance of Jesus to seven disciples besides the Sea of Galilee John 21:1-25

8th of 12 Jesus appears to the eleven disciples on a mountain in Galilee Matthew 28:16-20, Mark 16:15-18

9th of 12 12 Jesus appears to about 500 hundred people on a mountain in Galilee 1 Corinthians 15:6

10th of 12 12 Jesus appears to James his brother 1 Corinthians 15:7, Galatians 1:9

11th of 12 Jesus appears to the disciples with another commission Luke 24:44-49 & Acts 1:3-8

12th of 12 Jesus appears to the disciples with another commission Luke 24:44-49 & Acts 1:3-8

ABOUT THE AUTHOR

Dr. Julie Hitchens

Her written books are Heaven's Intervention On Earth, There Was Purpose in My Pain, Forgiveness Releases You Blessings and Command Your Day Spiritual Warfare. She is also Gospel Artist with a CD Entitled Joy Cometh in The Morning. She is also an acclaimed Bible Teacher, Prophetic Psalmist, Song Writer, and Pastor. Dr. Julie Hitchens founder and Senior Pastor of Joshua's Covenant Church and Julie Hitchens Ministries Houston, Texas, with more than 39 years in ministry. Dr. Julie is committed to souls for Christ. Her very existence is to bring the Good News of Jesus Christ to people of every color and culture all over the world, literally changing lives one person at a time. Dr. Julie Hitchens encounter with the Lord at age 3 and 1977 received the vision for Ministry. She is fueled by the love of the Father and His compassion.

www.juliehitchensministries.com

Dr. Julie Hitchens

www.ingramcontent.com/pod-product-compliance
Lightning Source LLC
LaVergne TN
LVHW021623080426
835510LV00019B/2737